[handwritten inscription]

Appalachian Ground

Lisa Creech Bledsoe

More poetry, wildflowers, and mountain at
AppalachianGround.com

Table of Contents

I. Property of Salamanders

Call the Mountain

Call the mountain, and she will come
with green-shadowed hawk
and salamander

Feel the land drop away from your feet
and fly
the song of all things, even
wild cherry in August,
bear sign and
the praise of bees

Call the mountain, and she will billow
in on thunder and
white slants of knife-rain

You will be a vixen bolting
for her hole,
the scent of lightning
stinging her nose

Ask the mountain to attend you —
this thing can be done, and will
with savage gravity
and the ordinary hush of moss on stone

She will adjure you to
the work of the land

You will be wind-seethe of grasses over balds
benedictions of the vireo
ghost of elk and red wolf

Then
you can let your leaves give up
and fall

Night Message

The same darkness rises above every house, and the same great moon. I have set out across the field to ask what music is left in the season, to let the hard white starlight blink out its flashlight message.

Lying on the earth, I listen to the ticking of the weeds until my body is filled with gray night clouds; in the nest of dirt and leaves between my collarbone and ribs hums the small wild mink of my heart.

Maybe we are here because it was our plan, or maybe we were called here by the deep green song of owls, or the flickering wing of a cabbage moth. Either way, the past breaks open and ghosts move along our paths.

Here is a thing worth doing: Let your thoughts be turned under like a garden at the edge of winter. Heap wet black leaves and compost over your spirit to encourage whatever gifts and riddles will grow there in secret.

Much has died and is gone, but like the two of us, the wild violets will grow their white bones and threads all winter in the dark forest soil.

Broken Into Wholeness

I waded into the creek today
to sling blackening clots of leaves from the snags

I rebuilt my stone crossing
prying up rocks from the silt and minnows
and laying them like careful plans —
with a care for the black-shelled snails still attached

I am not ready for summer to end

The water is still warm and the color of tea in the sun
but the creek bank is lined with yellow leaves and
puffs of milkweed
the bleached skeleton of a possum or raccoon

Everything is larger than we are:
    the current, the seeds, the bones

To give our full attention is to be broken into wholeness

Emotional Clearing

Today is a good day to rearrange your emotional furniture.

Better yet, drag that chest of drawers — the one filled with neatly-folded grudges, tangled slights, clumped frustrations — out of the room of your heart.

Shove it off the porch and let it crash its way down the mountain and into the startled woods.

A year from now, or ten, it will surprise you as you wander through your inner forest. A mouse will have made a home in every drawer. Wrens will have woven your old insecurities into their nests, and honeysuckle will have turned your grief into fragrant cups for bees.

The glass knobs from each drawer will long have come loose and tumbled into streams, dazzling the salamanders with sun-sparks and rainbows. Your anxieties and unforgiveness are leaf litter.

Do this each year, and lay afterward on the open expanse of sun-drenched hardwoods in the home of your soul

and breathe.

Song of the Spring Beauties

I intended to try them this year
foraged and harvested wild
enjoyed in a salad, or cooked

And in March they emerged in thousands,
scattered drifts of pink and white like
confetti at a wedding
their tiny round roots — fairy potatoes! —
a flow of elfin river pebbles under the rimy mulch

After a dragging winter, how bright
these fair faces flushed in the rugged wind
their rosy stems and green leaves glowing

An unrestrained anthem
on a muddy, frozen mountain at
the end of the firewood
the end of bleak sky
and shivering

Seven years
it takes for each bloom to rise
from seed to rousing chorale,
ripened beauty

I went warm-wrapped with bucket and trowel
but gazing out, became rooted:
an antiphon in celebration of this
slow mastery and small wild praise

You and I need these here — all of them! —
feeding the psalm of the world

Winter Love Poem

Walking up the mountain together in the watery sun we
saw two bright male cardinals and a small, fast female.

We watched one energetic Romeo pursue his intended.
He flickered and dipped, following her with zeal
through the tangle of bare apple branches.

The other male sat glumly in the briars. We walked
right up, our hearts laughing and sore at the same time.
"Get in the game!" you called. "Take it from me; if you
don't try, you can't win."

I love the way you can so easily throw open the
windows of my heart under a winter sky.

Found

Sometimes you are chosen
by what you have not sought.

The boundaries meant to contain you
are upended by a thousand years
of hard frosts and soaking rains.

Every green and black summer —
every dragonfly drifting over swamp milkweed
remembers the things you weep for.

Your griefs and wounds are kept in soft mud, then
folded into the crease of the mountain
recorded in slate, schist and quartzite.

The unfurled universe claims you and
presses down her favor.

The white spruce will never forget your name —
he spells it again and again in unhurried syllables
each taking years to sigh.

The wrens and veeries will sing
down the darkness creeping up your twigs and
ligaments, and
you can not be unhealed.

There's no escaping this.

You cannot tell the fiddleheads to rise but not unroll
or remonstrate with the roots of yellow violets
gathering their strength for spring.

Your platelets and spinal cord
your salty bones and neurons
are the property of salamanders and colona moths.

You have so amazed the blue crawdad that
she has spun you into bright embroidery for the seep
and that isn't done quickly
or without effort.

You are a map of light, a river of electric charge,
juice and gravity and tectonic plates shifting
the voice of a thousand bells.

You belong to all the earth and even more.

Open palms or clenched fists
bowed head or raised
the blessing will find you
and when your resistance is finished
it will carry you tenderly home.

Slough Stone

in the fragrant bowl of the slough

wanders a path I carved
into the steep shoulder of the mountain
down to the end, turning

then a long walk straight into the middle
through all that loves the wet, sodden
loves the sliding mud
to the tree bridge, which you must cross
to get to the other rim-path and out

ahh! the tree bridge
one ragged root-end on the firm
a stretch across the slickery stream bed
to the branch end in the redolent, mud-glut center

the branches are all rotted and gone and
in several places the log is half slunk in mire

no matter what
your boots are going to get sloggy and wet

but I have in mind — my secret! —
to carry an ample, weighty stone
to the middle of the slough

a thundering mother stone
lush with lichen
splendid and wide-hipped
enough to offer a lift
over sludge and muck to the log

it takes a while to find the right stone

again some time to debate
and look some more
before prying the winner —
the most fair and exquisite rock you ever loved —
from the fist of the mountain

and (this is the crazy part)

tipping it

on edge

somehow

steering or...

(watch your feet)

getting it down (surely not up!)
the mountain without
losing hold or getting (much) injured

then wrestling, of course
the runaway stone
from wherever it lands

hauling by pure stubborn and rope
to the path, the end, the center
smearing sweaty hair back
hands and haunches aching

but
what
a stone!

the matchless ally to lay before the log bridge
a muddy, scraped offering
(which has gouged a ragged path) but
a splendid step (just think of it!)

until

the sinking
digestive slough
claims this mass too
and tree...

but not yet!

you must
my friend

be willing to entertain reveries
on your mountain
of the biggest, most sublime stone you
can almost hold

convince everyone
to help you in your labor of love
ignore words like absurd or pointless
revel in the artistry of your choice
the perfection of your calling
the way you two found each other

then make a thousand journeys

a hundred thousand steps

together

while you can

New Things Born

The coffee-colored creek
is foamed with white this morning
the mountains wreathed in leagues of silk

In this damp coolness
this place where the sky rises and
the earth yearns to follow
new things are being born

Trees have begun to drop their seeds
to the sodden ground

Hard green buckeye husks are turning dark and soft

I know less than the water strider
less than the crawdad turning in the clay
but I know this

From root to crown we are changing

Siege of Crows

I was dimly aware of the crows as I climbed. They vexed and scolded and beat the air with wing claps as I made my way up the switchbacks.

At the top they were seething in one of the great boundary trees for no reason I could see. The understory is more open at the ridge top; the deer den down below where there is cover. Up here there are only the venerable trees and yellow violets in sun-shot gloom. And today, a siege of crows.

As suspicion arose in me I stopped moving, feet stitched to the ground, breath frozen. The birds nettled and spewed.

Suddenly a murky shape exploded from behind a beech and launched itself across my path and down the mountain, contours blurred with speed and unmistakeable power.

For a moment, I knew the scent of a predator and my small rabbit heart seized with clarity.

> *You carry the mark of blessing. You have brought the tender creature you are to the wild place you were called. You cannot be here unfaithfully, no matter what you think.*
>
> *You walk in light, trailing shadows and roots.*

May the damage you've done to yourself fade like the deer's hoof prints in the muddy slough: they fill with water, glint a moment in the sun, then disappear.

Go now in peace.

The crows fell gradually silent, shaking down their feathers and staring at me, trembling in the wake of the coyote.

Scarlet Elf Cups

Below curtains of fog and sullen rain
a spore sinks its creamy fingers into the crumbling rot
and blooms in the black slough.

As if a grinning sprite has overflown
and dragged her sparking feathers in the sludge
with no other thought but playful delight
without even opening her eyes but here!
and here! and hidden here
the scarlet elf cups erupt
and lay winking in the mire.

You should hunt them too.

Lace up your sturdy boots
call up the cats and go into the woods
and fill your eyes with secret rubies.

Who else in your life will venture out in the muck
and find treasures no one else will see?
Will your ghost go, when you have failed to live?

Go before it's pleasant and warm.
Hope for once for a dismal rain —
days and shivering days of it, if you can.

Be greedy for the days and places no one else chooses.
Look especially for dying trees still standing
piles of sticks softening with decay
and tangled, rotting weeds.

That's where your soft scarlet gifts will wait for you
each one glowing.

Advice

"That's nice, darling."

If you have an inner saboteur, this is what she tells you. Sometimes you'll be hard-pressed to discern the sub-surface malice.

"…But maybe you should leave art to the artists."

Ahh, there she is.

(Her sly, faux-positive comments about me to everyone else have been redacted, but think vanilla-cream cupcakes infused with strawberry-scented hydrogen sulfide.)

Time to check back in: I've already gotten what I want. In the slough, with the shepherd's purse in bloom, the voice of the creek and the offering pool.

The rest — recording it in a way that catches the filaments of light on the water, or reminding us both of a promise and a power we forget so easily…

(You are chosen. You are connected.)

…is windfall. The sweetest fruit blown down from the top branches. And maybe a rotten one now and then; those come off so easily you know. Pick it up and polish it on your sleeve, or leave it and keep walking.

This is not about cinquefoil or speckled trout. The place where you find sublimation — or discomfiture — might be a duplex with a concrete floor and a wooden desk. It might be a suburb dotted with recycling containers.

Go ahead: run your fingers along the fringe. Your place may be extraordinary. Your place may be desecrated. Claim and explore the outer and inner landscapes. It's all holy ground.

And it's not true that you should only write about what you know. Try writing about what you imagine. Try tropes, understatement, folly. Build yourself an inner gothic mansion and live there. (You're gonna love folly; it's one of my favorites.)

Try missing your mark as much as you possibly can. Walk as if you can't see, can't smell, don't know that there's a giant patch of bee-filled honeysuckle… Right. There. Write all around it without touching it.

Remember the old game of molten lava? Stay on the path or you'll be consumed! Then sigh dramatically, give your final speech, and leap with abandon into the flowers. (You may get stung by a startled bee, but that's the price of art.)

Fall in love with the words! There's no need to be strait-laced about this. I never met an adjective/adverb I didn't wanna get frisky with. You're allowed to embolden, wander, reek, galvanize, outrage, bore. You can divulge it, retract and squelch it; cringe, sigh, wallow, grin. Be bombastic and quotidian. (All words I'd date.)

Do it for yourself. Leave what everyone else thinks in
the refrigerator to chill. (See what I did there? If
nothing else, this proves I'm hip.)

The critic inside you will say what she wants. Let her be
heard, but don't let her rule. You be the czarina. Or the
secret love interest, if you prefer. Or the crowd
vigorously waving their handkerchiefs as the handsome
soldier departs on the steamship.

Isn't this fun?

Night Work

The moon tonight is a golden door, nearly shut. It has snagged, I think, on the sticky knuckles of the great spruce. Maybe on cloud laundry. It will shut soon, but I will still hear the murmur of lovers, the muffled thuds and whispers. Although that might be the bear, snuffling and groaning in the slough. She will have cubs but is not yet denned down for the winter.

The black mud sucks down the bones of the deer buried below the starlit ridge. The bones become seeds: we are stained and softened and fit together into new shapes, to wait for snow to harden us.

Put down your plans and concerns. Allow the face you don't show to be devoured by the dark field and the secret sages who chew and ferment the soil. You are art, and creation. You are infinite love. This is the marvel of the night.

II. Hive Songs

Rescued

wearily I stumbled downstairs and
before coffee grumbled against
the piles of dirty dishes waiting to be washed
both sinks full and the counter

while water heated for coffee
I moved dishes from sinks
into increasingly unsteady stacks
and at the bottom was shocked

to see a half-drowned, miraculously uncrushed
honey bee in the drain basket

my heart started and rushed

coaxing her with the care of a surgeon
onto my washrag, checking wings, legs,
thorax, antennae
she was so quiet and still
where in her body did the stories reside?

snapping off the gas under the teapot
I carried her gently into the cool morning
the restorative sun still high on the mountain and
wouldn't reach the house or bee yard for two hours yet

I thought of the time my grandmother
popped her daughter's half-drowned chick
into the gas oven and in ten minutes
everyone recovered

as a 6-year-old hearing the story for the first time
I was equal parts horrified and thrilled
remembering how close it had been for
Hansel and Gretel
and hugged myself in relief

coaxing my bee onto the wide porch rail
I pointed her in the direction of home
hunted up a fresh, perfect tulip poplar bloom
in case she needed nectar
and went in to not wash dishes some more

ten minutes later I heard a familiar buzz
and climbing interestedly along the side of my
pajamas printed with giant red strawberries
was a still-wet but happier bee

equal parts baffled and delighted
I carried her out again
to the poplar bloom on the porch rail
but she sailed steadily off instead toward
the lime-colored trees where the sunshine was glowing
up the morning mountain

Listening For My Life

For so long I was a stranger to myself. Now I am
sending out new roots, learning how the trees talk to
each other, parsing the language of the crows. I have
become a student of the black vultures who came to
show me the deer kill, and the crawdads who clean the
spring.

Today, the thrush!

Her casual mastery of song, dappled breast, and wings
carving a scoop of round blue sky. I am listening for my
life, remembering how to sing.

I fold these moments carefully and lay them on the
small shining altar of my heart.

Neighbors

Pan told me about a black snake
who lives peaceably in an opening above her door

Once she saw this snake
at the threshold of her den
gracefully lower a length of elegant neck
to allow the bees who shared her refuge
to walk on the bridge of her spine
inside

Perhaps it is as the poet said —
"Your love lifts my soul from the body to the sky"

This is the work of snakes and bees
to make of our differences a bridge
between us and home

Bluebells

This spring we discovered
while walking the rim of the slough
a startlement of bluebells
flung against a steep decline.

They had almost escaped notice
being so nearly the color of the deep shade
beneath the witch hazels and
young buckeyes hunkered there.

Together we cut a careful, winding path down and past
in order to better enjoy those dusky gifts
next year, should they reappear —

but at the bottom met mud
and a stop to our path.

A tree had collapsed across the creek
and unable to flow down,
the backup had drenched the meadow
leaving no way to cross
but through the muck.

Even together we couldn't
lift that ruined trunk from the creek
and great handfuls of rotting wood came up
with each try.

The hatchet worked better,
splattering us both with mire but
slowly exposing the bright heartwood until
the creek began to run over and down again.

It was later that we got the call.

Their son was the same age as one of ours.
It was a violent death.
No words serve.

The hard-built path ends where the meadow flooded.
The bluebells —
so sensitive to disturbance —
might not return.

And the great tree will lie across the creek
for many years yet,
with icy spring water slipping through
the notch cut deep into her heartwood.

Blueberries

I have conducted an inventory of the blueberries
on the mountain above our house.

There are precisely one hundred and ten:
sixty-five on the highest bush,
forty-five on the middle bush,
and on the low bush, disappointingly
none.

When it comes time to eat them I shall count them out
slowly like
the woman in front of me in line at the supermarket
counts out the change from her pocketbook
painstakingly, double-checking.

One should be careful with one's allotment of
blueberries.

You can't just leave them in a bowl on the table
or they might be dumped on oatmeal (all at once!) or
casually tossed in the air and caught in the mouth —
or dropped!

It's painful to think about, these blueberry
misappropriations,
these failures to savor.

A single tiny cobbler could be made, and shared.
One spoonful for each of us.
Oh, that crust, that steaming plummy scent —
such intoxicating sweetness.

One tiny bite of midnight sky for each of us —
one deep azure ocean surrounded by cinnamon sands,
a moment of spaceflight and weightlessness…

The silhouette of the man I love
walking toward me down the mountain after dark,
bringing me one hundred and ten blueberries
as a gift.

Haven

Sitting in bed under the open window
I have just begun to see fireflies
beyond the moon-limned eaves where the bats moor

Then a deep gray bending, shuffle
of takeoff and landing
warm wing, flutter
quiet turning, plitter
past the glow of my book light

Pouring in and out
like flour in a bowl, hushed
they slip, gather, fall, inhale
sail
through the tumble-dusk

We won't close the roof cap until
the pups are weaned and flying
late this summer

For now I listen to their mothers
alight, rustle, enfold

You and I search the same night sky
but see different things

Close your eyes and
sing your way forward
wing your way up
stream through

There will be new homes
in these woods in autumn
roosts, forage, haven and
the forest will welcome you

To My Crow Friends

You, I know, because you never forget a face and names hardly matter.

You're no villain. I see you swooping over the clearing after the hawks, but you let our one timorous owl stay (he keeps quiet and doesn't interfere with the Family).

It's your intellect I admire; you see how to puzzle up the water and you are willing to carry stone after stone after stone. That's the story, anyhow. Plenty of open water here.

I saw you once, furtively looking about before stashing a treat (is anyone watching? this is only for me), but to guard your future you'll choose tools over treats.

So yes, the enviable mind and sugar, the variable dialect! You fit in, you do. Come visit me up here on my porch, honey (just leave my bees alone).

I'm not the first to lean on you for spook factor; you ruffle and shrug it off. But still you gather in a mob around a deceased loved one, never touching, and never returning to that place: death-mystery is strong there, and requires reverence.

They do say in the city you bring the blackouts. And drop your walnuts into the street to be cracked, waiting for the light to change before swooping in to peck up the treasure.

You have treasure here, too: your glinting white bits of quartz, a spent shotgun cartridge, a blue Lego. My silvering hair is twined in your nest and I don't know if that's bad luck or good.

Good I think, because you returned the lost lens cap, that charm, and two dead voles (those weren't mine actually, but thank you nonetheless).

Your parcels and parliaments, your hovers and hordes, your musters and storytellings.

You, I know.

Winter Hive Song

Walk slowly up the mountain to the bee yard. Every step counts toward wholeness.

The snow is sifting down like sugar beneath the poplars, and the electric fence ticks in the hush. I click it off, then unhook each line, leaving only the lowest, which I step over.

It's too cold to open the top to see if they've eaten the sugar cake I put in there last week, on a rare warm day. There is so much I don't know. This rattles inside me like dry sticks.

Kneeling in front of the hive, I shake off my gloves and put one bare hand on either side of the box. The clouds of my breath rise: one, two, then a third.

Nothing.

I wait, then close my eyes and lay my cheek against the wood.

The hum rises against my bones, and my heart blooms. The hive sings, and I know the bees will find me.

When you are looking for the center of your life, you don't have to be good, or know exactly how this is done. The way is different each time, anyhow.

Walk slowly up the mountain to the bee yard. Every step counts toward wholeness.

3 am, The Cats Want In

sschup sssshupp

Our paws fit nicely under this door.

ffit ffit ffit

If there were something to snag
we would have it!

rattle rattle

Can we come in?
The dog is in,
why can't we can't be in?

thump wump wump

We won't eat his food again,
this time we promise!
It's tasty, but not as delightful
as an almost-dead chipmunk.

yyyouuuuuwlll

Did you get the almost-dead chipmunk we
left for you downstairs, a few minutes ago?

scrabble scrtch scrtch scrtch

Hey! You're up!

Vixen

I see you, tame woman
blundering through the woods to the creek
your mind flapping like an injured crow
resisting the implacable journey of day toward dusk.

Let me ask you a question:
Do you hear anxiety in the creek?

The leaves fall, turn to silt, more leaves fall.
Bones and roots, bits of chitin, a deer
all the moss and jewelweed, of course.

Will the creek be used up?

I see you, tame woman
never quite making your case
pushing back against gravity
trying to find the thing to which you belong.

Here's a wonder for you:
Do you hear the creek quarrel and contend?

The summer leaves shutter her view of the sky
but she sees the stars every winter.

Will this happen again?

Here, watch me and you will see what to do:

41

Crouch and wait for the twitch.
Pounce and dig into the wet belly of the creek.
Snap up the crawfish.

Sometimes you do not get one.
Most times.

But when you do it is good!
It is enough.
Now go home to your den.

One Thing Becomes Another

I put banana bread in to bake
lace up my boots and
hike out amid great shafts
of afternoon gold

The ironweed is nearly gone, but
goldenrod has exploded like fireworks
in the field above the house

The scent of woodsmoke and forest mulch
go well together —
one thing becomes another

Imperial Moth, Adrift

Last night we left the shed light on
so you lost your way

For generations your bodies have only known the moon
for navigation
and the stories take so long to change

Buried alive beneath the snow and leaf litter
your genes blazed their way through winter
dissolving your digestive system
building reproductive magic in its place
until the summer night crooned you awake

From the last of your births —
      your final magnificent decay
you emerged the color of a yellow moon
elegantly furred and feathered
to the ancient family of royal night sky sailors

You no longer have the choice to eat and remain

You breathe only
to hunt for a female in whose flame-bright wings
you could burn
to gift the sky to a new generation

Tonight you must fly or fail

Time consumes all things but it is
the children who are lost
in an age of lights that are not moons

You have been led off course
the secret cargo of your progeny
abandoned in our sheds, adrift in our nights

Such a short, precious time we are given

I walk on the mountain as the dusk flutters down
wash my hands and face in the offering pool
and ask forgiveness

The Ladies

One always arrives first and
lets the others know

Scrutinizes the preferred patch of weeds
sauntering over and back
graaack-graaacking mildly
but at consequential volume

I crack one eye to peer at the clock
resolve a five and wish for a six

She trumpets censoriously and
I put a pillow over my head

By six the ladies have all arrived
and are well into session
peaceably and resonantly reporting
the placid happenings
of their morning so far
and yesterday's, this week's
the summer's
so far, again
in serenely coarse splats and
gobbets of repartee and remark
sleek black plumes ruffling
over such delectable palaver
outraged not one bit

I have coffee
finally
and walk down barefoot
to let out my little dog

who races down
and bothers them
not one bit
although they have lusty and
stentorian comments —
offspring running
uncivilized through the place —

And when it is time, not before
the ladies will rise with pomp
piercing skaaarcks and gabbles
and leave the floor to the
silly wrens
and finches

III. Star-Swallowing

Seven League Boots

In fourth grade I learned the beauty standard
as we stood in a tight circle, one foot in
to be strictly evaluated

Small feet, miniature steps
were to be most desired
employing the least space possible

It was best to be
hardly noticeable

And far too late for me
tallest girl taking
giant steps that made my ponytail bounce

I dreamt of wider strides still
in seven-league boots
surging across vast lands
over ogres' lairs, enchanted marshes
roofs of thatch and goats and gingerbread
across boundless black woods

With a hunger that is the beginning of everything
a body built with heft and hip, muscle and volume
prodigious baskets of provision, salt mills
magic tables laden with secrets
never ending

Feet wide and well-shod in streaming fathoms
hair raveled with clouds
a wool cape the color of spruce
shot with garnet
hawk feathers and moss

Seek your fortune
not to find princes, gold spindles, or sevens
but to feel the rooms of your story
empty, then replenish themselves

Open locked closets
chatter your stick against the fence
leave river stones upended, constellations askew
and see the shades you fear eclipsed, worn thin
and cast across the land like tenebrous blooms
known, and known, and known

You are not too hungry, generative or vast
There are never too many curiosities in your pack

Wend, wander, fly in your great boots
trailing bright streams of light, and
refuse to relinquish the sacraments
of speed, weight, and wonder

Wild Tea

Crown me with wild rampions
give me a robe of scratchy grass
and yarrow for a scepter

You shall be my knave of shovels and secrets
our joker will wear a motley of moth wings
and slime mold

How is a crow like a poem, does anyone know?

Now. We'll want tea and stones
with blueberries, if the deer have left us any

And a dappled bower
(Whatever's dappled will do
as you've always loved dappled)

I found three black shoe soles in the creek
which should serve for platters
and bee balm along the drive

May as well invite the surly toad from the spring box
but ask him to keep his voice down
and bring buttercups as
we'll be needing lots

Kittens! Clear out these mouse skeletons
before I pour

(Never mind plates for them as
they'll sleep through the rest)

Pass the milkweed, if you will
then we shall all move one place on

Bluebeard

i.

There is rot spilling down from
the eaves of the world
the landlord painted over it but
you have seen the wasps coming and going

There once was a lovely man
but strangely his footprints left behind
traces of sodium cyanide and the sweet scent
of almonds

I'm sorry you were taught to be nice —
there is much to unlearn

ii.

If you use the key and turn over the rock
        cut the string around the shoebox
        drop a torch into the well

If you examine false promises of freedom —
        unlock any room except
        eat from any tree not including
        be yourself although

If you ask, expand, breathe
on the coals of your curiosity

Be ready for
shadows to deepen and multiply

blood to roar

There is nothing you may not see if you look
and one day you will tire of the knowing

The door can be shut but
the key will continue to bleed

iii.

They said it was her brothers
who saved her but
I have seen a woman laid low
by many a rattlesnake and live

It is imperative that you learn to
disobey the predator

More than one wisdom lies within you
More than one bloody key

iv.

When it's over again
hold back a portion of the poison
a pinch in your pocket to keep your blood wise
a dusting to code your knowing
crumbs that once marked your pathway home

Apologies

Thank you so much for the invitation but
I have to count the leaves on the three-leaf clovers
wrinkle the periwinkle, and
repeat the day's directions to the wind
(who never listens)

Before noon I'll have oiled the salamanders
sharpened the crickets' saws
and fluffed the hummingbird hatchlings
(I go through so many cotton swabs)

I have to arbitrate between the crows
who are forever pilfering each other's teaspoons,
draw dots on the tiger lilies that haven't any
and turn down the temperature in the spring
for the crawdad boogie tonight

And by then it will be late

There's winding the bees
reminding the owls to update their journals
and new sheets of grass to be scissored
(I ordered perforated, but they're always out of stock)

Trust me, you'd be shocked
at the number of acorns
for whom I must crochet caps
(they'll all be mauve this year to avoid
the fuss over who gets what color)

And much later I'll

unplug the fireflies for the night
and set the heat lightning to intermittent

Otherwise I would love to come

Star Rise

There once was a woman who swallowed a star

That may not have been exactly what happened, but
it seemed likely something inside her collapsed, then
flashed up her bones and
light spilled from behind her teeth like
a lantern in an old barn

At night it was most strange

She lay on her back under a sapphire wheel of night
wishing to lift away but
the broomsedge and switch-grass held her with a
sharp-edged lightness and
the checkered beetles stitched down her edges

Three times she threw off her heaviest ballast —
a fourth was too much and she took it back

It mended poorly but there was nothing to be done

As the years spun she became a constellation

None of the thirteen in the daily paper
but something imperative
still streaming into place
not hydra, not maiden, not bear
but storied, certainly and
pressing, dense and luminous

In the old tale the stars
became coins and fell

But perhaps instead we open
the field of light beneath our faultlines
and let our silver rise

Earthsnake

Somewhere here there is the story of a snake
the color of a silky dirt road
a beauty of cream and brown
sinuous as a woman's hips
sleek as your lover's collarbone

she smells of wild sage and ancient history

she never asked for your forgiveness, and
what she longs for she never shares

just flows silently to her burrow
a river riding over stone
sand poured hand to hand

she dreams of clouds beneath her belly
and nestlings on her feathered breast

she'll be here when you are gone

delicately tasting the green-scented air and
polishing her copper heart until it gleams

The Dirty Shepherdess

It was once said —
and it was only said once —
that I had a pretty face

Grimy and ragged, though
those words have been used plenty
and I've certainly been windburned
sweaty, and stinking more
of rotting mulch, woodsmoke, and forest cat

> *bread and life*
> *a ring, a knife*
> *salt, flour and water*

I prefer practical of course
ingenious on occasion, and
I can fly like a bird when I need to

My feet are suited less for crystal slippers
than a mountain trail or stony riverbed
I can manage an ax
start a fire, scavenge shelter and
turn a loaf

I'm not above subterfuge
if it gets me further along the path

> *bread and life*
> *a ring, a knife*
> *salt, flour and water*

If certain people were quicker on the uptake

outrageous hints —
 a gold ring against the knife,
 a wedding feast with no salt —
would be unnecessary

And it was never true what they said
that no other woman could wear that ring

Rather than thinking what a stroke of luck
you could say what a lot of suffering
could have been avoided or
what a resourceful woman

  bread and life
  a ring, a knife
  salt, flour and water

Would you still choose apples over salt?

Plenty of those legendary beauties are filled
with sorrow and a radically altered future

With a world at stake
a pretty face is fine but
we all need salt to live

Foundling-bird

They are not making a mistake, you know —
mothers, being sewn
into the hems of their children

A hawk's nest is never a good place to leave a child

They become yours and
you forget their wild origin,
their savage nature

It isn't long before the stitched
and restitched tether
begins to tear

Of course it hurts —
strong thread pulling against
pine needles and the small, sharp fish bones
which have become embedded over the years

Sometimes there's a sudden yank and sundering
the muscle memory of stoop and dive
a burst of feathers and warm blood

One day you look down and your heart is
terribly damaged but your own again, mostly
and will heal

If you resist becoming a rosebush, lit and gleaming
a chandelier in a church, or
a bonfire to consume the great black forest

That light only reaches the bird in
stories told by others

Instead carry water, pot by pot
powdered comfrey root and agrimony
barrel by barrel

Become a pond and when
the witch comes to drink up the water
you must drown her without hesitation

Leaving

You were born on an island
like we all were

Kept in a fur-lined nest or
locked in a windowless tower between
sky and earth

When the food runs out and darkness presses
it will break apart who you were taught to be
from who you are meant to become

You must dig your way out
with your only small knife

There will be more death and destruction
than you expected
and ogres all your own as well

Good things die
and every bridge you cross
will exact a toll

You must renounce and escape again and again even
things you love or are comforted by

Turn a deaf ear to being told you can't do this or
do this and no more for you have no tools
no strength, no time

Compliance will not conquer your enemy
Being nice will draw leeches that
must be clawed off by force

Exchange timid teachers
for wild ones and around those
guard yourself

Learn to separate seeds from soil
needles from stems
poison from water
not to prove your worth to those you left behind
but to shiver into

The story that awaits you

The Mute Swans

It isn't true that we never speak

Doesn't our name sing?
Do we not love our children,
our little lullabies?

We have never returned home for
the things we've forgotten
landed on windowsills or tapped
on the windows, all of which
would be ill fortune

Though fate and fidelity
are in the eye of the witch, one might say
and she has found us reliable
or is playing a quiet shell game of her own

The rude *izba* at the border of the land of the dead
has a stove of solid Russian works; what a nest
the roof makes
if you don't mind the grief and howl of
death at your back

Or, of course, the trophy bones —
fancywork, fuel, sorcery of life
and Yaga the shaman
with a blazing skull in her closet

If you are quite clever
you might win the use of such a talisman
but it is best not to cut your fingernails or
wear anything new when you petition her

Bring rye bread and apples for us
or a fat silver fish
but nothing under a spell (we have enough of that)
and in return you might find us inattentive, dizzy
or having an off night

It isn't true that we never speak

But you must pull your own weight, child
find the brother you lost and
build your own disenchantments

All Night This River

Open the enamel box
underneath your ribs
and draw out the white locket
whose chain is a river
whose river is you
and you the ferryman
deckhand, river horse, naga
filled with fish wisdom
belly full of gold bullion, legal papers
and a sink full of dishes

All night this river
rises and rolls
rises and falls
There are boundaries to your landscape
but not limits

Lift the orange salmon sun
from the roof of your bonehouse
where it weeps and gilds
your leaps, sleeping and climbing
and you the satellites
stars, stings, centaurs
planted in the blue garden of night
for your nine good deeds
hummingbird eggs
and a dozen pint jars of honey

All night this river
rises and rolls
rises and falls
Cross three times the watercourse

over, back, over
and find yourself in a new place

Break from your frozen moraine
the great stone who dreams of flying
cracking the old songs into fragments
and you the grinding slab
the marzipan ice wolf
turtle, lullaby, snowfall
hunting the glacial till for
black jewels carved into crows
shist, then shale
then silt in the firth, funnel, door

How small you shall become
before you belong to the sky

Five Maps

I've made trails with small white stones
breadcrumbs, buttons, omitted commas
pressed pennies, and paper fortunes

I gave away
a box of handkerchiefs sent to me
singly, over years
by my great grandmother and her sister
laced, embroidered for a
girl becoming a woman
I gave away all the
pink depression glass, too

Now they narrate a different land
with cotton lawn, silk, and
engraved remembrances

I've made trails with
blackberries — wait,
I ate those
but the seeds, the seeds
mark something, or will
— with blackberries, virgin's bower
blue crawdads, cornbread
scuffing the leaf duff
and chopping in a path with my
round-point shovel, sometimes
a mattock

And how many leagues have
flown along the page,
busy-tangled, sleepily rumpled words

charting trumpet weed and territories
hunting and shining
owls, bowls, and petals
on how many pens and sheets!

Today I sat and watched the erratic
flights of bees, making no
sense and perfect harmony
their own algorithm of sticky love
and hive-ness

So many small cherished maps
are folded away in my pockets
and cabinets, along the lining
of my shelves and tales
including this one

IV. The Storm and Home of Us

Cabinet

Inside my chest is a cabinet
of a thousand drawers

With them all shut for company I'd say
it would be tidy except
for the constant leakage and
the strange grinding sounds

The drawers rattle open on their
own no matter what I do
and randomly cave, coalesce, incinerate or
cough clouds of spores

Inside an entire row at the front
(it's important to tell you this right away)
are layers of brown confidence in
thick sturdy pages

Though one day I will have
filled a dozen sheets with charcoal drawings
and the next the drawer has swollen shut
and refuses access

Some drawers are stuffed with wool socks
and baby bonnets
beeswax and the amiable natter of crows
a few blazing fast starts (not many timely finishes)
the sweet perfection of cleanly splitting a chunk of
beech on the first swing

Row after row have stones under which there are
salamanders

But there are also tiers marked *need to please* and
overthought
(I scratched through the labels but
you can still read them)

The ones dedicated to precision I've never opened
(smashed the edges with rocks — didn't budge)

And the paint is lovingly worn
from *untethered*, and *deeply attentive*
and *the attenuation that comes*
with gradually being spun into a glittering stream of light

Released

For weeks I called the cutleaf toothwort by the wrong name. It niggled at me, then suddenly I realized where I'd gone amiss.

It bloomed all over the mountainside anyway.

I remembered a moment back in our pale February — I was stricken to find a wildly curling orange and yellow bloom erupting along the bare branches of a tree like fireworks.

"What is it!" I demanded, both elated and baffled.

Mary Jo told me, of course. "That's an Orange Squiggly with Eyes." And it was.

Just for today, you could let go of your need to be perfectly correct. Drop your guard, quiet your heart, and allow things to unfurl without your nomenclature.

Watch for the things that germinate, or effloresce. In the name of the Carolina geranium, you are forgiven. By the power of the squiggly witch hazel, you are forgiven.

You are living energy, made from stars, and cast wildly out again.

Tonight, despite your efforts to prevent it, the deer will nibble at the tender young shoots on the blueberry bushes, and trample the false earthstar into clouds of spores.

The Storm and Home of Us

You were born, I think, like a storm precipitated from
the breath of the thousand generations who came
before, created of ancient queens and charm quarks,
hippogriffs and wood sorrel.

Hiking into the woods after a spring rain, I feel the
salamander turning lazily in the mud of my genes. Did
you know she is suffused with homing metals that call
her to the water? When the sun shines, her body
becomes a glittering flame that loves the puddle, the
pond, the great river.

So there is magnetic dust in my gut that compels me to
slide bare hands beneath a clod of sodden leaves, to
turn over endless rocks in the creek surging down the
mountain. I am looking for home.

We are warriors and red algae, feldspar and manticore
and garden mint. We are made of clouds and etched
with holy meridians. Wave by wave our lives are called
to their source in rushes and rivulets until the last burst
of fine mist, then cloud again.

Cherry Tree

I have been studying the space between fear and grief.

Last night before the moon faded, I climbed up to stand under the dying mountain cherry.

Nine stone steps, slick with unease, then another short rain-soaked rise. I can see into our second-floor bedroom window from here.

Thirteen nights more until the man comes to take down the tree; a feat that will involve harnesses in neighboring trees and a careful system of pulleys and ropes. The cherry is a hundred feet tall, three trunks splitting away from the main, badly rotted at the base.

Death leans toward the house.

Thirteen more nights, and sixteen inches of rain so far this month; nearly four times the average. I rearrange the numbers over and over again, but they aren't my numbers, over and over again.

Sometimes as you are carrying your laundry up or down the stairs, you will forget.

At night, in bed beneath the moon-shadow of a dying cherry, you will remember.

Shut the bedroom windows so that you can't hear another inch of rain, or the whip of wind. Turn off the flash flood warnings on your phone. They aren't your numbers.

Stand in the slippery weeds with your palms and forehead to the tree. Allow yourself to grieve and fear, fear and grieve.

The sharp, liquid arrow-song of the wood thrush will leave a silver scar on your heart.

The Church and the Wildflowers

I do not believe I must choose between
the church and the wildflowers
between the Apostles' Creed and washing dishes
while my son does homework at the table

You can learn much about God from
a weathered marriage or
a bouquet of blue asters and goldenrod
gathered from beside the gravel drive

The world is a great banquet,
tables set not with embroidered linens and
polished silver
but with coffee cups and some spring violets

You and I have done nothing to make this happen
but we can choose to be present, curious, glad

For it is possible that our lives depend on it

It is just possible that our lives depend on our presence
and rapt attention to the Great Feast in our kitchens
on our mountains
with the people and creatures
both lovable and reviled
already gathered where we are

Hit and Run

Sometimes your heart needs more space to do its job.

You know those calls you get, where afterwards you stand clutching the phone to your chest and holding back tears? That's three for my year, so far. How grateful I am to still have my son. It can go either way, you know. The great tides sweep through our lives, triggered just as easily by the act of choosing between loaves of bread as getting into a car.

When you draw close to a miracle, you sometimes catch a glimpse of the waves of horror and weeping against which miracles are often born. How tempting it is to build an understanding of life based on what hurts, or what's missing. One despairs of human fragility.

Instead, turn your face toward life, despite its constant proximity to death. The lone root still breaks through the stone, the single stone still changes the voice of the river, and the one river continues to shape and refresh the world.

Boxes

In a small box knit of moss and a murmuration of birds there is a wisp of duck down and a red jade Buddha from the day he was born. The stink of cigarettes and the resistance of the world around me I sprinkled with wild mint and rosemary for a holy fire.

I had made the box earlier for the whispered name of a different child. The unsaid prayers and shorn locks of a saint I folded into bright origami frogs to scatter in the woods. The crows carried them back to their nestlings as toys.

In the small box woven of larkspur and icy spring water there is a generous twist of pale blue thread, the kind surgeons use to cross-stitch two hundred sutures into a four-year-old's head. My grandmother washed the blood-drenched winter coat (twice) and I shook out the down for birds' nests and sewed a thousand sky-blue sails for toy boats.

He doesn't remember much of it, smiles easily, and isn't afraid of dogs. I don't love them any more.

In a small box shaped of lichen and bits of eggshell there is a chunk of quartz carved into the shape of a deer. The terrible phone call and the hospital smells I mixed with dish soap and glycerine, and later we sat on the front porch to blow bubbles, letting the sunshine heal.

For the next terrible call I cut a new trail into the mountain to the offering tree. It seems to be working so far. The thin folded shadow I may look at in 20 years, or never.

Make ham sandwiches, hunt for salamanders in the creek, and tear the dark thoughts into strips for your bee smoker. This winter there will be honey.

The Offering Tree

halfway up the ridge, at the top of twelve steps
not really steps, just hard mountain dirt cut into shelves
there is an offering tree

I've left there curls of grapevine
nuts, a yellow violet
broken snail shells

yesterday there was a wide acorn cap
not mine
with the rest, rearranged

a moment of startlement
nothing like the hook in the chest
you get as you parent

when your children pull the cable
thick as your wrist
which you would love to disconnect

not really though
but you've chewed at it in misery
wished it less firmly anchored

you are a tree fallen in the woods
with small gifts left
by hands you love

you cannot roll away
from their hidden dark glory
the futures you cannot protect

Ablaze

Coming in together
at the close of day
we surprised a young ringneck snake
soaking in the last of the sun

Seeing us
she slipped behind the steps
to hide under the deck

Of course we followed
both of us on our knees in the dirt
whispering like excited teens
hunched over
inching deeper into shadow
to catch
a glimpse of silk and cream
softly folded into a crevice
between stone and ledge

We quieted
sensing each other's heat
and felt the secret unfold
like we have years before
and many times since

Breathless
ablaze in wonder
as night dropped her cloak

Moving Stones

Yesterday I stopped
trying to be useful and
wandered out to the creek

Where the wind had not yet
come ahead of the rain
and there was no need

To haul stones
and thump them down
in the mud again
for a crossing

The sun licked her thumb
turned one more page
then gathered up her yellow hem
and still

I moved stones
in the purpling woods
rearranging my thoughts
with the pileated's
periodic commentary

Some things you will do well
Some stones you must leave unmoved

The stream sighs and gleams
under a swelling moon
and the rain soon
will sing her compline prayers

One Year

It's a good day for a house-iversary and
there are presents for everyone —
though the bears I've left out
for good reason

We've made cakes in the shapes of
little chocolate homes
with no leaks, new gutters, and all the
damage torn out and repaired
with peanut butter frosting, delicious
and wildflower sprinkles in every color

For the crows a thimble, boot, top hat
polished to a glittering shine
race car, iron, wheelbarrow
secreted in the moss
(I lost the cowboy)

A handful of cornbread crumbles
scattered in the creek for the crawdads
and celebratory rockstacks
to be enjoyed by all

Five silver spoons
(my great-grandmother's)
filled with and spilling honey
at the seep for bees

And the kittens — a year old now!
have a new white ribbon
dangling from the doorknob

There's one fluttering on the ridge as well
which might capture the bobcat's gaze

Under the boundary tree
for the coyote I've left
my best, trickiest riddle

And there are ten well-washed
grapes on the neighbor's property
for the raccoon
with a line of cat food showing the way

The wild cherries, goosefoot, ironwood
hickory, ash, witch hazel, well
there are as many hugs as can be arranged
yellow buckeye, beech, maple
one hundred fifteen thousand heartbeats of gratitude
today especially
for winter heat, green summer shade
and the deep, fragrant
breath of the woods

And finally
the deer receive forgiveness
for eating my blueberries;
next spring I will plant more

V. Maps of Light

Clearing the Seep

Late in the afternoon I went out to clear the clots of leaves from the seep, where it threads down the mountain into the pool we built for it not far from the house.

Snow is coming in tonight but right now the sun has a golden ferocity that calls for a surge of deep-hearted work. I find the round-point shovel, then dig through the box for my yellow deerskin gloves, the ones that are so agreeable and supple, and fit me better than they do the men I live with. In the clearing below the house the crows are arguing amiably.

Heading out of the shed my boots crunch on muddy gravel; tomorrow it will be icy and treacherous. The wind is already churning through the trees like a kettle coming to boil. But for now there is sharp pleasure in dragging away the matted slags of black and ochre leaves until I can see the last of the light glitter off the water as it trickles down.

I dredge the leaves out of the pool, then sweep the muddied water along the channel with my shovel until it finally tips past and slips down the mountain, all surge and tumble and perfect satisfaction. I watch until my ears begin to burn with cold.

Sometimes your path is so clear and keen it aches. Sometimes — just for a moment — your way is bright as molten copper burning its way down, reflecting the cup of the world as it runs. Even the earth is inflamed and swept along.

Back at the shed I put away my shovel, then gather up an armload of wood to build a fire for the night. It's dark inside now, but I do not yet want to turn on a light.

To Life

When light floods down
in the temple of the woods
there is work:
bright chemistry of sugars
simmered, bloomed, perfected
freely passed and shared
stem to root
from the holy cup
swallowed
in great draughts

And the leaves say:
> *let us drink together*
> *let us dry the cup*
> *may you be delivered to life*

The tree is blind to one color
which is laid aside
trundled up to the roof
tipped out the windows
kept out of the way
of the busy kitchen and
long table of the leaf

How blessed we are that green
  — sage, emerald, viridian, pine
is of no use to the tulip poplar
shagbark hickory or yellow buckeye

Now breathe and
bathe in the sanctuary of green
birch and basswood

and love well the gift

And the people say:
let us drink together
let us dry the cup
may you be delivered to life

Spider Flight

Sixty miles out to sea Darwin
looked skyward and saw silver
filaments fringing every
rope aboard the ship

Spiders fly because they are pushed

Not wind
but charge propels them aloft

Every day along the edges of the planet
four hundred thousand storms
brew and prowl, crackling

Skyships amass
thin fire strikes and
sleet hisses down

A spider turns her gaze to the earth
stands on tiptoe
and spins up a thread

Electric stormjuice squeals
and streams

Ions careen earthward
are repelled and

Eight delicate feet
hundreds of thousands of tiny contacts
with grass, twigs, roofs of the world

Vanish

Are bounced
into green winds
to fly
toward unknown lands

Ode to Brown

cinnamon, nutmeg, loam, dusk
beans, molasses, gingerbread
oatmeal, rye bread, rolling pin
toasted sesame seeds

a weathered wooden boat, jump rope, apple butter
old paperbacks crumbling in the attic
my father's boots

mushrooms, pecans, homemade bread
dried cornhusk dolls we brought home from the Ozarks
a hummingbird nest, tiger's eye

the prickly sweetgum balls, stepped on barefoot
rotted plums from the neighbor's tree
nightcrawlers, dried blood, Coca-Cola in glass bottles
a pond the cows have been in

gravy, biscuits, pralines
the wren who sat on my grandpa's shoulder
my mother's Volkswagen Rabbit, first car I ever drove
my worn-out basketball

hot tea in Mussie's Haviland china,
Ohio River Flood of 1937 and
the sepia-toned photos of people who lived and loved
through world wars

the smooth skin of my grandaddy's housemaid,
and our last president

the kitchen carpet at Graceland the day Elvis died
empty locust shells we hung in our hair
rough speckled muscadines slowly covering the
abandoned house in the woods

round pebbles at the bottom of the Spring river,
paddles, faded life jackets
the tarp draped over the canoe that we slept under

crickets

my carved cherry bed
the metal bookcase in my room,
with all my Nancy Drews

my little sister's chifforobe
Bonnie Bell lip gloss in Tootsie Roll flavor
root beer barrels, Milk Duds, Twix bars at Halloween

lizards, snakes, salamanders
School shoes, hush puppies, peanut butter
Nutty Bars cost a quarter in the lunchroom
the ribbon in my Heavy Metal cassette tape, re-wound
with a No. 2 pencil

my boyfriend's thick, wavy hair

Stuck

once I wandered
into the woods and discovered
a secret cave which sighed and
stirred the hair on my neck

I found the cave because I wandered

yet

in all the wide world
there is a strange phenomenon
in which I allow a single pebble —

any random small-focus point, really

to not only serve as editor and critic
but also a sucking black hole
a lockup

I focus on this and nothing else

in all the wide world I allow
one small

      — cannot even name

to decide what I am to do
where I will go
what I may or may not express

I have only the tiniest cell in which to pace
and I have gone there myself and

infuriated
locked myself in

this is how wandering ends

what we do to ourselves

this is how we miss
the secret caves in the woods

Thresholds

This may happen to you:

You may have an orderly house built in your heart, yet be unexpectedly, powerfully distracted by thresholds.

Doorways shine so hot and blue I have to shut my eyes and turn away.

Or go out, of course.

If you go, you'll find yourself dropping your hands and saying "I just don't know," then listening to the sometimes ridiculous, often profound secrets the water has to share. You'll miss meetings because of this, and have no excuse.
You might be taught by the most unsavory birds, and become known as a lover of weeds.

After a while there won't be much left to recommend you any more, no clarity or cleverness. You'll be a fool who lingers on the fringes of burnt places and ruins. You will curse and bow in the rain and stand amid an argument of winds. The land will tease and trick you. But if you take off your shoes, it will tolerate your feet.

You'll be an odd friend to an unpredictable power.

It will be more than this. It will be enough.

On the Last Small Bouquet of Gentian and Boneset

I had saved this for you these past weeks
or perhaps for myself

Thinking, there may not be any more this season
or the next

Then today on my walk there were
fragrant mosses in citrine and jade and amber
leaves with their thousand songs
and burning filaments of light
quilting the surface of the creek

This is how we become who we were meant to be

Not by clinging to a few bright gifts
but by letting go and having them all

Riptide

dreamt I was
standing on the beach when
a wave reared up
and dragged me impossibly
out to sea

breathless

a woman gulped my name
roar of a towering whitecap
coming

and — !

knew what to do

slipped under
satin black leagues beneath

terrible sharp-toothed birds of the deep
howled but
fed them stones and stones

waited

for the wave to thunder past

then winded
aligning my salt-light body with the shore

began

the oblique journey back
thinking of book signatures, bees, woodfires

you know what to do

wrap your fear in stones
angle toward the shore

the brine in your blood
knows what to do

There Will Be Days

There will be days during which your heart feels like an
abandoned house at the end of a long gravel road.

You shouldn't go there, but you do, furtively. Anxiously.
You have no business there, but the trash and detritus of
squatters — a mattress, empty tins, worse — these call
for a witness.

What you don't expect, of course, is love.

To be ambushed, laid low, crushed to the grass by the
intoxicating scent of muscadines growing wild.

The clicking (what? what?) of your stuttering heart —
or the cicadas which have climbed out of the dirt after
seven years in the grave, croaking in astonishment.

This is the beginning of grief, this place of shattered
glass and exposed boards.

Or the awakening of love? Is that it?

So hard to distinguish between them, and possibly not
worth the effort.

The Same House

Does the steadfast root tell the leaf
Be still and do not pull so in the wind!

The leaf shivers and laughs
at the root's imperious command

She chortles in response
You, root! Why don't you bump and sail the sky
like I do?

The tree loves them both and more

You, leaf, will visit your older sister
after the throat of the snow carries you down
and the wild wood conveys you
piece by piece
vein and flame
into the bright singing under

We live in the same house but
we will all be changed

Measured

Today I added myself to a flash flood warning
a mudslide, and thirty sheets of honeycomb
pressed into frames.
I can't open the hives in this downpour but flowed onto
a page of washi and a handwritten poem.

I became a cherry tree two hugs wide
dying and holding on,
the ash leaning above the seep,
and five black locust skeletons streaked with rain.
Silvering into mist I pooled among the pines
with three other women whose sons all suffered.

You and I want the same things:
To know the worst and be free of it.
To sustain the terrible wounds and still sleep like a wolf
with her nose on her paws.
To remember our infants with their peony heads.

We must break ourselves into equal birds,
into seven shining stones in shades of slate
and jet and jade
ten little eggs
four promises

reduced in the end
to a galaxy with a thousand suns
falling into our hands,
still burning.

Begin Again

I was satisfied with grocery-store bouquets until I
discovered wildflowers. Now I know how the strong,
dappled leaves of hepatica live through the winter, then
die in the spring snow to make way for one perfect
bloom with the sheen of a pearl.

The suburb kept me until I saw a spotted thrush return
each afternoon to the same mountain meadow, singing
until robins filled the long grasses to feed.

Now amid yellow buckeye, trillium, trout lily, and the
parliaments of crows… The way creek song changes in
pitch after a rain? I can never go back.

The threads you painstakingly knot together each day
unravel. Holding lovers, molding sons, repairing and
hoping. When you are sewing the world together there
are more broken pieces than whole.

There will come a time when you unhunch and unfold
your aching hands. Stand on the worn wooden boards,
the cold cement stoop, a patch of dirt — maybe a little
grass. Just stand until you remember the ground will
support you.

Stand for a month or four years.

The wild turkeys will feed on wood violets while you
wait, and the birches will raise your children. Drink
your tea, the towhee will urge.

Then a honeybee needs to be rescued from the seep, and you will need to find a twig. Take your time, this is a test. This is how you will begin again.